REDUCE, REUSE, RECYCLE

Rebecca Rissman

WAYLAND
www.waylandbooks.co.uk

Published in Great Britain in 2018
by Wayland

Editors: Paul Mason, Elizabeth Brent

Design: Peter Clayman

ISBN: 978 1 5263 0117 8

10 9 8 7 6 5 4 3 2 1

Wayland, an imprint of
Hachette Children's Group
Part of Hodder and Stoughton
Carmelite House
50 Victoria Embankment
London EC4Y 0DZ

An Hachette UK Company
www.hachette.co.uk
www.hachettechildrens.co.uk

Printed and bound in China

Picture acknowledgements: All images courtesy of Shutterstock except pages P7: Getty Images/Zing Images; p13: Getty Images/Christian Science Monitor; p15: Getty Images/Thony Belizaire; p19: oconnelll/Shutterstock.com; p21: Getty Images/Arpad Benedek; p27: Getty Images/Tony Robins.

CONTENTS

EARTH IN TROUBLE - HELP NEEDED!

Rubbish litters the ground, smog hangs in the air, and giant islands of plastic waste float in the sea. Earth's environment is in trouble. But it's not too late. You can help!

You have probably already heard about pollution. It is the name for harmful substances in the environment. Some of Earth's air, water and land are polluted. Much of this pollution comes from human activity, such as driving cars and operating large factories.

POLLUTION AND GLOBAL WARMING

Our pollution contributes to global warming – the slow increase in Earth's average temperatures. As the planet gets warmer, it is affecting our weather and climate. There has been an increase in droughts, and more extreme weather. Global warming is changing Earth's ecosystem.

In 2015, volunteers picked up rubbish from beaches around the world. They kept track of what they found. Many of the items they collected could have been recycled.

Rubbish washed up on a beach in Vietnam.

FIGHTING GLOBAL WARMING

People can fight global warming by reducing pollution. Because making things causes pollution, making fewer new goods will help. Reusing old items, reducing the number of new things you buy, and recycling as much as you can, are all ways to do this. These simple steps can be very helpful, and can reverse some of the harm done to Earth's environment. They can also help to prevent new problems caused by pollution.

TOO MUCH RUBBISH

People create a lot of waste. They throw away old food, plastic, paper, metal, glass and much more. The amount of waste we create is causing problems around the world.

Rubbish is bulky, smelly, and sometimes dangerous until it can degrade. (Once it degrades, rubbish can become part of the soil again.) Some rubbish – for example, batteries – contains harmful substances. So rubbish that is not safely contained can pollute the habitat of living things.

Some rubbish degrades quickly. Items such as apple cores and used tissues break down in a few weeks. Others take a very long time to degrade – a glass bottle can take up to one million years to break down. Some items even become toxic while they are degrading, such as certain plastics that release dangerous chemicals over time.

WHAT'S IN THE BIN?

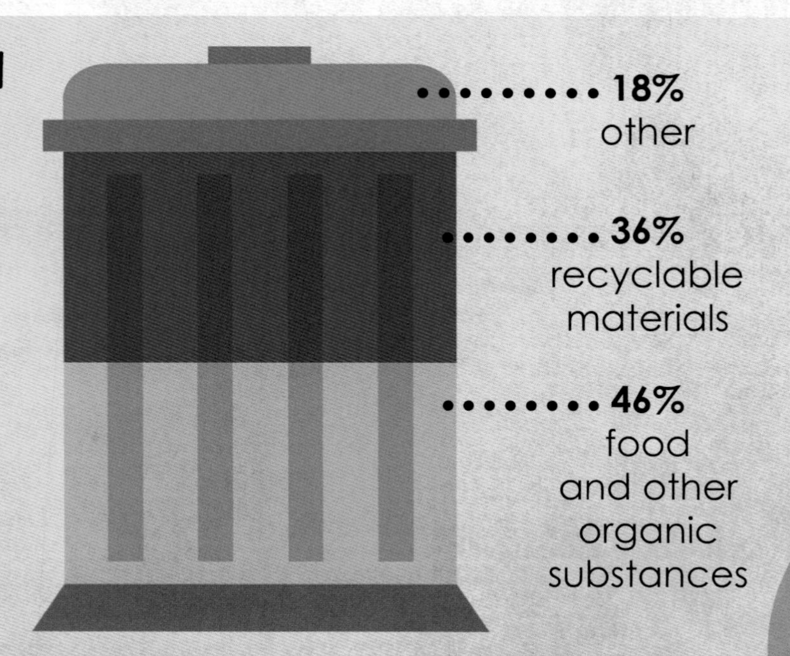

Much of the world's rubbish is made up of things that could be recycled.

Employees responsible for throwing away their own rubbish are often better at recycling it.

TINY RUBBISH BINS

Many people don't think about how much rubbish they throw away. In the USA and Canada, though, a simple idea is changing things. Office workers are given tiny, individual rubbish bins for their desks. They are also each given larger bins for their recycling.

When an employee's rubbish or recycling bin is full, they must empty it. The tiny rubbish bin fills up quickly. The larger recycling bin takes longer to fill. This makes people think about how much waste they produce, and encourages them to recycle more of their rubbish.

This idea has helped offices to greatly reduce their waste, and has increased the amount they recycle.

REDUCING OUR RUBBISH

How can you help with Earth's rubbish problem? Simple – just reduce your rubbish! There are lots of ways to reduce the amount of waste we create.

USING REUSABLES

Reusable items, such as metal water bottles, cloth shopping bags or ceramic coffee mugs help the environment. These items can be used over and over again, which reduces the number of disposable items that are thrown away.

Another way to reduce waste is to avoid buying products with a lot of packaging. Plastic bags, cardboard boxes and metal tins are all types of packaging. Making packaging causes pollution, so buying items that have more packaging than necessary is wasteful.

THE MAGIC MUG

NEW-OLD LONDON FASHION

London's East End Thrift Store is a hot spot for fashionable people interested in helping the environment. The shop sells only pre-owned clothes. These have been owned – but not always worn – by at least one person before being resold.

Charity shops and pre-owned clothes stores are a great way of reducing waste. People don't throw away clothes they are bored of: they give or sell them to the shop.

As well as reducing waste, pre-used clothes reduce the amount of new clothing that people buy. If you buy a pre-owned coat, for example, you don't need to buy a brand-new one.

Finally, pre-owned clothes stores reduce packaging, because the clothing does not need new tags, bags or plastic hangers.

REUSING OLD ITEMS

You probably already reuse things every day without even noticing. A water glass, breakfast bowl and toothbrush are all items you use over and over again.

Reusing objects doesn't only reduce the amount of rubbish people throw out. It also means new items need not be produced, packaged and sold. This saves energy and money, as well as waste.

Some items can be used many times for the same purpose, like a glass or a toothbrush. Other things can be reused in new ways. Sometimes, an old item can even be reused in a way that actually increases its value. For example, an old coin can be made into part of a necklace. This is called upcycling.

THE MANY USES FOR A JAM JAR

PENCIL HOLDER

FLOWER VASE

JAM JAR

SPICE JAR

SNOW GLOBE

Old items do not have to be used in the same way again. Sometimes it is fun to find a new use for them.

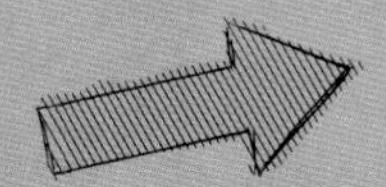

THE PLASTIC-BAG FEE

Each year, supermarkets in England used to give away billions of free plastic bags for shoppers to carry groceries in. These bags were often used only once and then thrown away.

In 2015, a new law was passed. It said that supermarkets must charge shoppers 5p for each plastic bag they use. All proceeds from any plastic-bag sales would go to charities.

This law encouraged people to bring their own reusable bags to the shops. It was very effective. In less than one year, English supermarkets reduced their plastic bag use by 80 per cent.

Laws like this have also been passed in other countries. Everywhere they have reduced the number of plastic bags in landfills and littering the landscape.

Plastic bags are a troublesome type of rubbish. They get caught in trees and litter the landscape.

RECYCLE AS MUCH AS POSSIBLE

Recycling – using the materials from old products to make new ones – is fast, easy and cheap, and has many benefits.

RECYCLING ADVANTAGES

Recycling reduces pollution: it takes less energy and materials to make a recycled product than a new one from scratch. It also costs less money to create goods using recycled materials. This means that in addition to helping the environment, recycling helps businesses and individuals to save time and money.

RECYCLING FAILS

Despite the benefits, most countries recycle less than 50 per cent of their waste. So why aren't more people recycling? Some say that they do not understand which materials are recyclable, others forget to do it, and still others think that it is too much work.

TIN-CAN POWER

Recycling 1 tin can ...

... saves enough energy for ...

... 3 hours of TV.

TRASH-FREE TOWN

The Japanese city of Kamikatsu used to burn its rubbish. But city leaders knew this was harming the environment, so they decided to change the way the city dealt with its waste.

Kamikatsu started a very strict recycling programme. People there must sort their rubbish into 34 different categories. They also donate items they don't want any more to a community shop. Other residents can come to this shop and pick things up at no cost.

Today, Kamikatsu recycles, reuses, and composts about 80 per cent of its waste. The remaining 20 per cent goes into landfills. The city hopes to create zero waste by the year 2020.

Sorting rubbish into different categories helps Kamikatsu to recycle waste more efficiently.

NASTY PLASTIC

Plastics are nearly everywhere you look. You might even be sitting on a plastic chair right now! Plastics are very useful – but they are also harming Earth's environment.

PLASTIC PLANET

Although plastic is recyclable, most plastic waste is thrown away, and does not biodegrade. Instead, it breaks down into small pieces which end up in Earth's water supply, being eaten by animals, and even in our food. Even worse, these tiny bits of plastic often contain harmful chemicals.

THE GREAT PACIFIC GARBAGE PATCH

The Pacific garbage patch is a huge area of rubbish floating in the North Pacific Ocean.

It is about twice the size of Texas and in some areas is 2.7 metres deep. It is mostly plastic waste.

Companies such as Thread are providing job opportunities and helping the environment at the same time!

THE MAGIC OF RECYCLED PLASTIC

The Caribbean country of Haiti has a problem with plastic pollution. It also has a problem with unemployment – many Haitians cannot find work.

An American company called Thread decided to solve both problems at once. Thread hired people in Haiti to collect plastic rubbish, which was then washed, shredded, and turned into plastic threads. These threads were used to make fabric for clothing, shoes and bags.

More and more companies are joining this eco-friendly trend. Fabric made from recycled plastic is so soft, you'd never know it came from a shredded plastic bottle. Clothes made from recycled materials usually have a tag telling you about their origin.

PAPER PROBLEMS

Paper products are easy to recycle. In fact, a single sheet of paper can be recycled up to seven times! And yet waste paper clogs our waterways and spills out of landfills.

THE COST OF PAPER

Making new paper – instead of recycling – contributes to deforestation, pollutes the environment and is also expensive.

New paper products are made from trees. Cutting down the trees, turning the wood into pulp for paper, and then cutting, printing, and packaging paper, uses a lot of energy. In some countries, paper mills have been responsible for releasing harmful pollution into rivers.

PAPER TREES

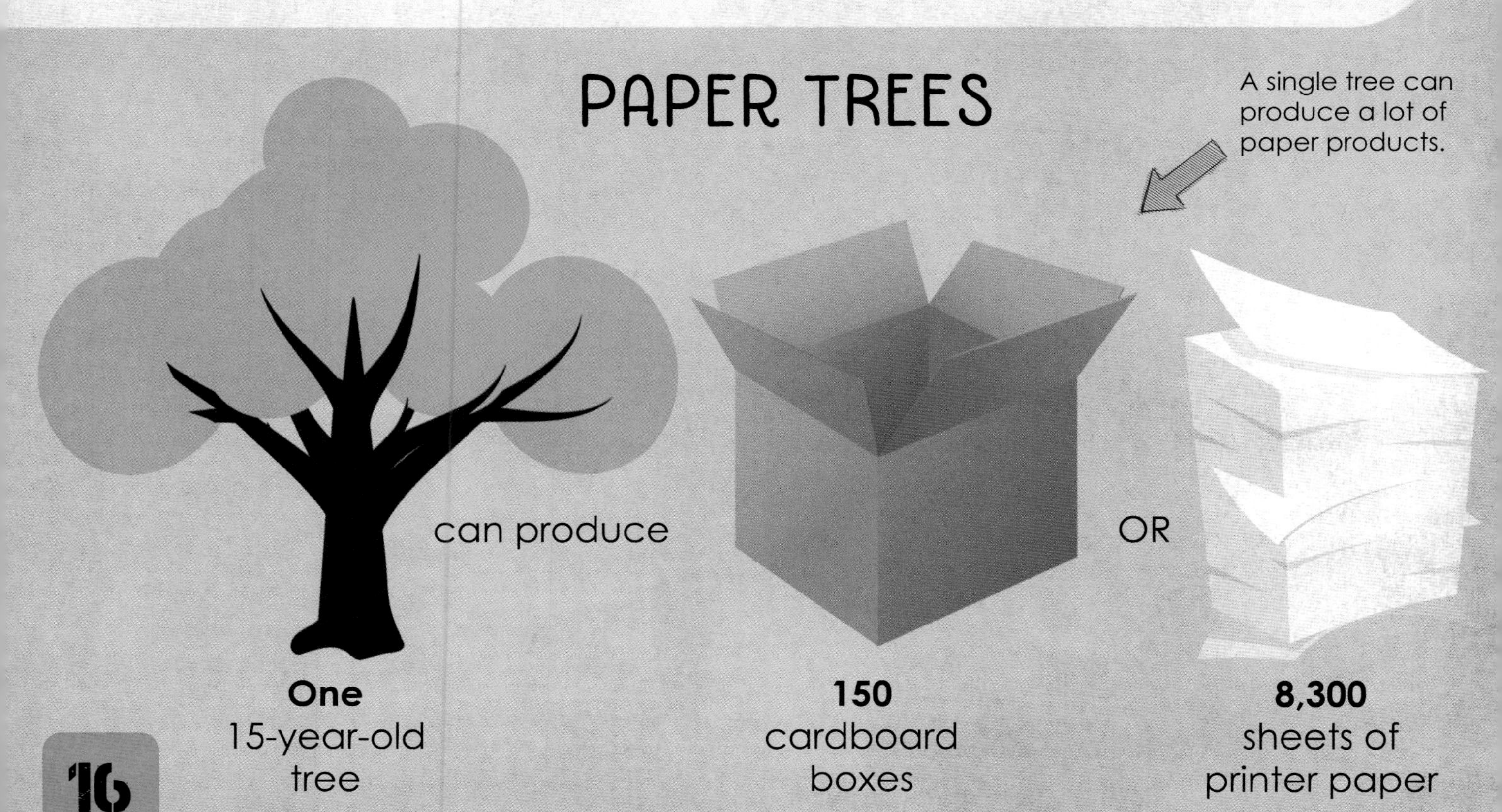

Going digital makes sense for many schools – students are usually very familiar with digital technology.

PAPERLESS SCHOOLS

One school in Scotland knew it was using too much paper, so administrators decided to do something drastic.

They went digital, scrapped their paper and pen routines, and gave each student a mobile PC. Teachers were given laptops.

Instead of taking notes on paper, students took notes on their mobile devices. Teachers stopped using paper handouts, and started emailing them instead.

This digital revolution was a huge success. It was popular with students and teachers, and the school saved money on paper and printing.

WASTED METAL

Next time you take a sip from an aluminium can, ask yourself how many times it has been recycled. The answer might surprise you. Aluminium, like many other metals, such as copper and steel, can be recycled an infinite number of times!

RUBBISH METAL

Despite being highly recyclable, metal still shows up in rubbish heaps and landfills. Each day, about 80 million metal food and drink cans are dumped in landfills – and that's just in the UK. Most of these cans are recyclable.

People sometimes say that they have trouble understanding which metal items can be recycled. Learning more about what can and cannot be recycled is a great way to help the environment.

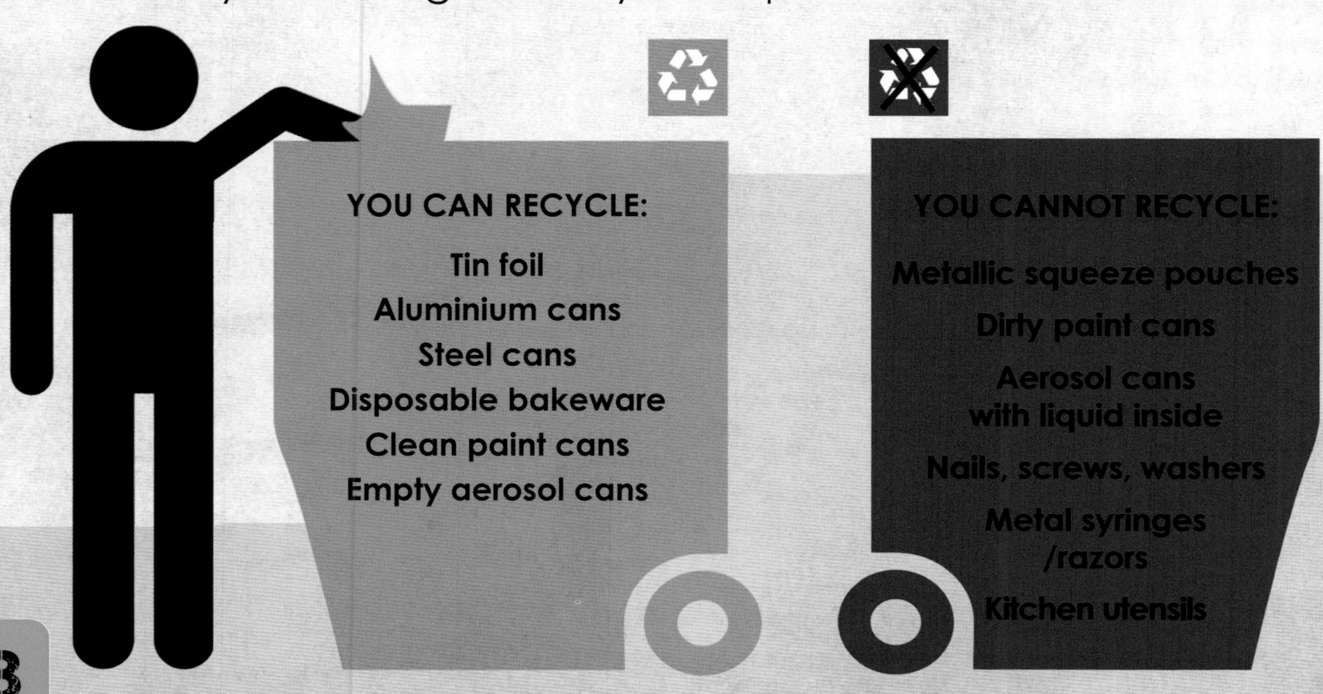

METAL CHALLENGE

The Aluminium Challenge is a yearly contest in the UK. It asks students to come up with creative uses for aluminium in three categories: transport, packaging and construction. Students from around the world submit their designs and compete to see who can come up with the most creative, innovative ideas. Winners go to a celebration dinner at the Birmingham Thinktank Science Museum.

The winners of the 2015 transport category designed an eco-friendly car. It is powered by batteries and solar panels. If the battery runs out, the team designed a pedal under the front seat that can be used to recharge the battery.

With a bit of creative thinking, recycling can be transformed into all sorts of things!

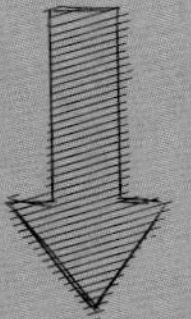

UK DRINKS CANS

60% are made from recycled metal

40% are not made from recycled metal

More than half of the UK's aluminium drinks cans are made from recycled aluminium.

GLASS IN THE BIN

Toss your used glass jar into the recycling bin and mark your calendar. In just one month's time, that jar may have been recycled into a completely new product!

Families in the UK use about 500 glass jars and bottles every year. When glass containers are thrown away, they become a problem for the environment. Glass does not degrade, or break down, so it takes up space in dumps and landfills. Broken glass can also be dangerous if it is not carefully disposed of.

Making fresh glass from old jars and bottles uses less energy and materials than starting from scratch. In fact, the energy saved from making one bottle out of recycled glass is enough to power a computer for 30 minutes!

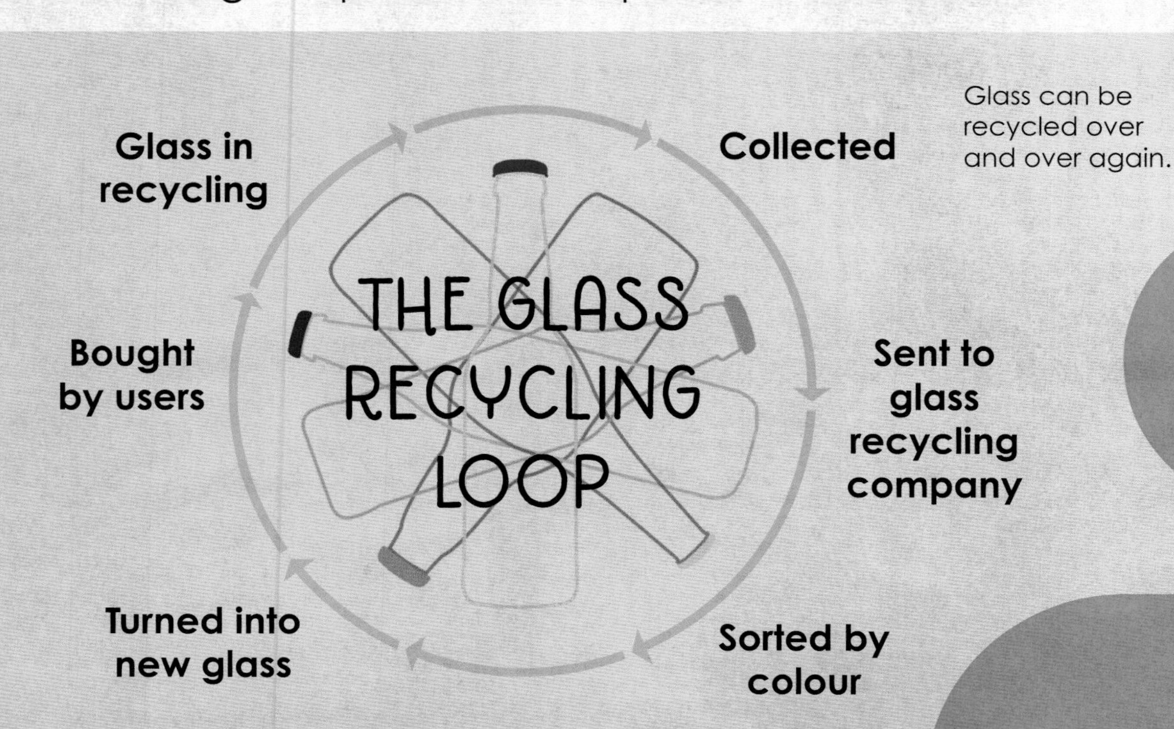

Glass can be recycled over and over again.

These glass bottles also add beautiful light and colour to buildings.

BUILDING FROM THE BIN

Most builders use materials such as wood, stone and brick to construct a new home. But a few innovators are getting their building supplies from an unusual place: the recycling bin!

Around the world, creative builders are using glass bottles, aluminium cans, old tyres and even plastic to build their homes. Some of these buildings are created to raise awareness or as public art pieces, but others are in use as real-life homes.

Tito Ingenieri, a builder in Brazil, has become famous for his unusual home. He built it from more than 6 million glass bottles he found in his community's rubbish!

FOOD SCRAPS

Food waste is one of the biggest reasons for Earth's waste problem. Food waste decays slowly when it is buried under other rubbish in a landfill. This contributes to the problem of pollution and overflowing landfills.

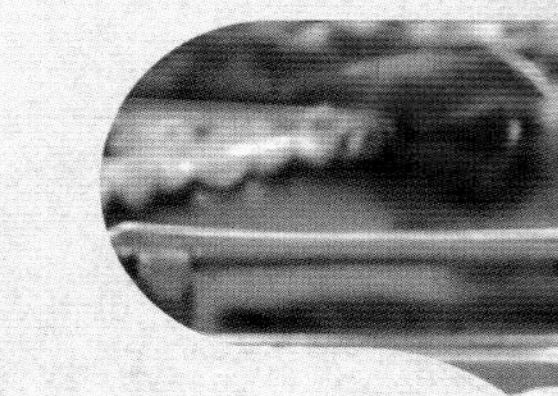

Hotel buffets are lavish and can sometimes be wasteful.

Food is wasted for many different reasons. Shops often stock too much of a certain type of food. If not enough customers buy it, the shop throws it out when it gets too old. Restaurants often serve large portions of food. If a diner doesn't finish his or her plate, their leftovers are thrown away.

Food waste does not have to be a problem for the environment. When food waste is composted, it can turn into healthy and rich soil, which can be used to grow plants. However, few people compost their food waste.

WASTED FOOD

Each week in the UK ...

... people throw out an average of six meals per household

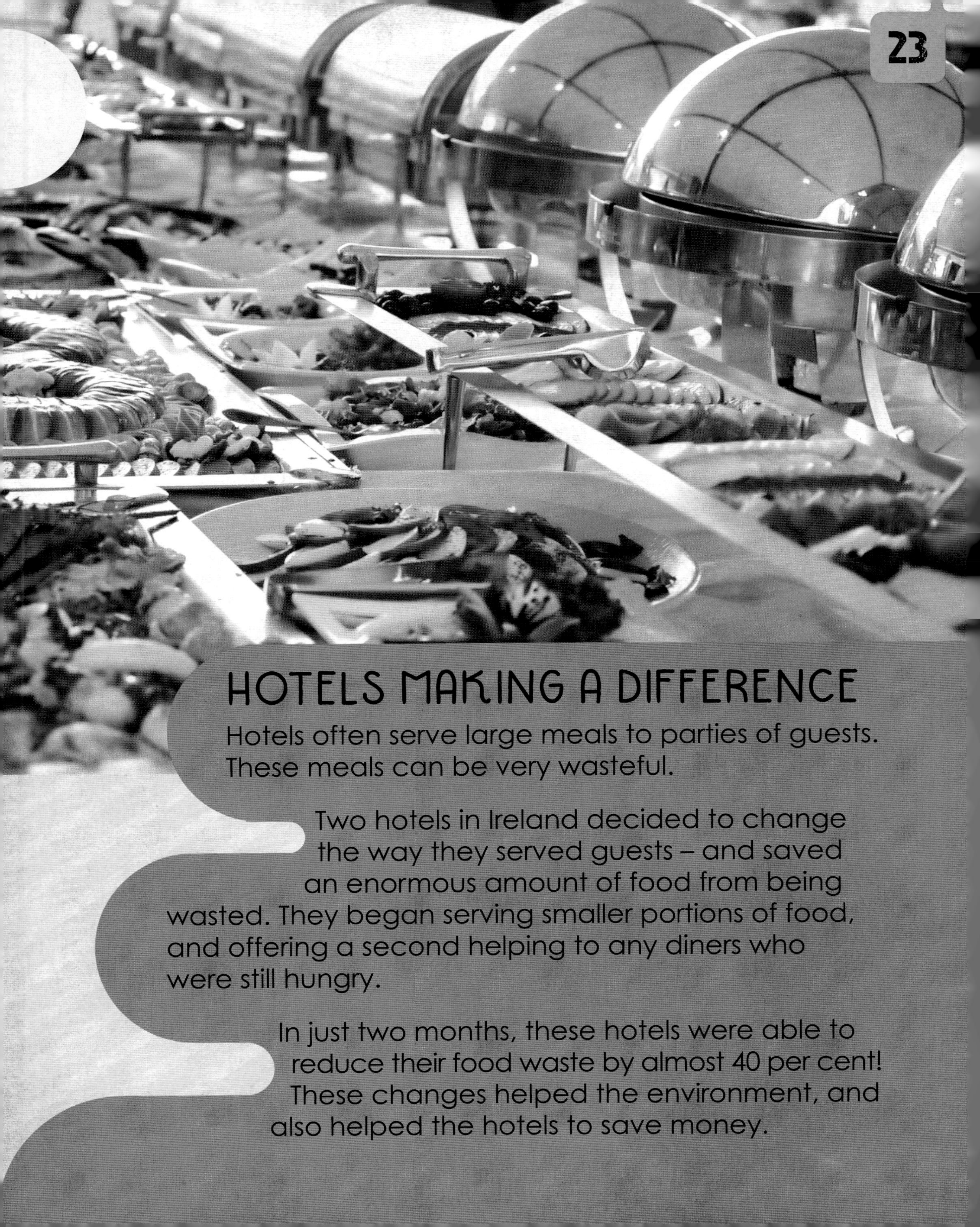

HOTELS MAKING A DIFFERENCE

Hotels often serve large meals to parties of guests. These meals can be very wasteful.

Two hotels in Ireland decided to change the way they served guests – and saved an enormous amount of food from being wasted. They began serving smaller portions of food, and offering a second helping to any diners who were still hungry.

In just two months, these hotels were able to reduce their food waste by almost 40 per cent! These changes helped the environment, and also helped the hotels to save money.

E-WASTE

What happens to your old TV when you get a new one? How about your mobile phone or computer? A lot of these items end up in landfills, contributing to Earth's pollution problem.

E-WASTE

E-waste is the name for electronic goods that are thrown away. Electronics are often replaced after only a few years, which means more and more are getting tossed into the bin. Dealing with e-waste is a growing problem.

Electronics are often small and difficult to break down, and sometimes contain toxic substances. Some recycling businesses buy e-waste, break it down, and resell the components that can be recycled or reused. However, this process is difficult and slow. This is one reason why much of the world's e-waste still ends up in landfills.

E-WASTE IN THE BIN, 2014

For every piece of e-waste that is recycled ...

... five pieces are thrown away

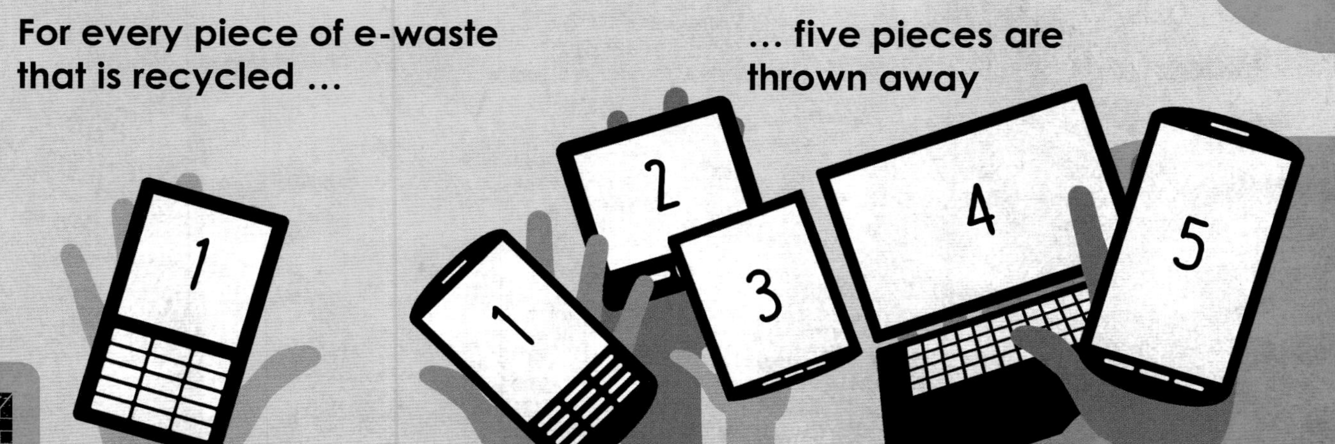

Old mobile phones that still work can be reused by people in need.

PHONES AND THE RED CROSS

Some charity organisations are working to increase e-waste recycling. Red Cross UK, for example, is helping people to recycle old mobile phones by making the process fast and easy.

People can either drop their phones at donation boxes, or send them straight to the Red Cross. The charity provides free shipping materials for anyone who wants to send their phone by post.

Charity organisations sort the donated mobile phones. Those that are still working are donated to people in need. Broken phones are sold to companies who take them apart and recycle the parts.

The Red Cross uses the profits from these sales to help people around the world.

WORKING TOGETHER

If you recycled all of your paper waste for a week, could you fill a whole bin? Maybe – but if your whole class worked together, you definitely could! We can do more when we work together.

Earth's waste problems can seem overwhelming. But when communities work together to reduce, reuse and recycle, they can fight some of the problems caused by waste and pollution.

The European Union, for example, has set a goal to recycle at least 65 per cent of all rubbish by 2030. They aim to accomplish this by enforcing new rules about separating rubbish for recycling, making it illegal to put biodegradable waste into landfills, and charging fees for waste collection. Around the world, other countries and organisations have similar aims.

RECYCLING ON THE RISE

In the USA, people have been recycling more and more each year.

2005
72.4 million tonnes

2008
77.3 million tonnes

2013
79.1 million tonnes

Restaurants that serve food in reusable containers help the environment.

OPERATION ZERO WASTE

Tamsin Chen wanted to change the world – so the 19-year-old from Singapore started Operation Zero Waste Dabao.

'Dabao' means takeaway in Cantonese. Chen had seen how wasteful takeaway food packaging could be. She knew most people used the plastic food containers only once before throwing them away. She understood this was harming the environment.

Chen challenged food vendors to change. She asked them to reduce the amount of plastic packaging they used on a local holiday called National Day. She encouraged people to bring their own containers for food on this day. Operation Zero Waste was a great success. It managed to reduce the amount of plastic waste thrown away on National Day by 75 per cent.

Chen hopes that people will continue to reduce their use of disposable takeaway containers in the future.

THINKING OF THE FUTURE

When you think of the future, what comes to mind? Do you imagine flying cars or hologram voicemails? What about a pollution-free planet?

New technologies are evolving every day that make reducing waste, reusing and recycling materials easier than ever before. These advances are coming from many different sources. Behind some of the best ideas is a massive range of people, from famous scientists to big companies and even children!

A company in India is making knives, forks and spoons that are completely edible. When you're done with them, just chomp them down! Another company, in the US, is making carpeting from recycled materials that cleans the air by trapping pollutants in its fibres! New, environmentally friendly products like these are appearing every week.

BIODEGRADABLE VERSUS NON-BIODEGRADABLE FORKS

Corn-plastic forks degrade in **30 days**.

Sugarcane-plastic forks degrade in **45 days**.

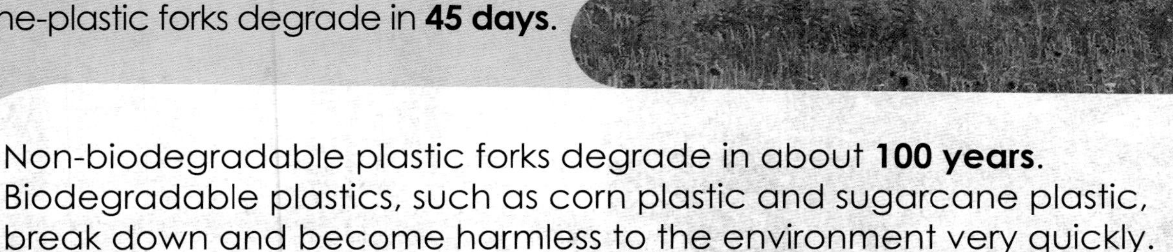

Non-biodegradable plastic forks degrade in about **100 years**. Biodegradable plastics, such as corn plastic and sugarcane plastic, break down and become harmless to the environment very quickly.

FAMOUS RUBBISH

In Northern California, in the USA, a giant white building has become famous. But why? It's the Sacramento BioDigester – the biggest waste digester in North America.

Waste digesters turn food waste into electricity, heat, fuel and other types of energy. Tiny organisms, called bacteria, break down the waste inside the biodigesters. They produce a gas called methane, which can be captured and turned into energy.

Biodigesters of all sizes are popping up in cities around the world.

The Sacramento BioDigester is a large, efficient energy machine. It converts nearly 100 tons of waste into energy each day.

GLOSSARY

bacteria tiny organisms that can break down waste

biodegrade to be broken down by living organisms, such as bacteria

compost rotted plants, added to soil to give it extra nutrients

component a part of something

deforestation cutting down forest and not replanting it

degrade to break down

disposable something intended to be used only once

ecosystem a community of living things that interact

fibre a fine, thread-like part of a material or a carpet

habitat the natural home of a living thing: for example, a whale's habitat is the sea

infinite endless

innovator a person with new ideas or ways of doing things

landfill a large outdoor area where waste is piled and then covered or buried

methane a gas that is produced when some materials decay

pollutant a substance that pollutes

pollution harmful substance in the environment

smog a mixture of fog and pollutants

solar panel a flat panel that absorbs energy from the sun's rays in order to generate electricity

toxic poisonous

upcycle to reuse something in a way that increases its value

waterway a water-filled channel, such as a canal or a river

FINDING OUT MORE

WEBSITES

Learn more about recycling at this helpful site: www.recycle-more.co.uk

Check out the U.S. Environmental Protection Agency's interactive website to learn about recycling. You also get to try your hand at being mayor of Dumptown! www3.epa.gov/recyclecity

This video can tell you more about sorting waste: www.bbc.co.uk/education/clips/zqm76sg

Learn more about Kamikatsu here: https://www.youtube.com/watch?v=eym10GGidQU&feature=youtu.be

FURTHER READING

Go Green! Join the Green Team and learn how to reduce, reuse and recycle
by Liz Gogerly (Franklin Watts, 2018)

What Happens When We Recycle?
by Jillian Powell (Franklin Watts, 2014)

Rubbish and Recycling
by Stephanie Turnbull (Usborne Publishing, 2016)

INDEX